Walt Disney's DONALD DUCK

• A BIRD IN THE HAND •

DONALD MAKES HIS ESCAPE, BUT IT ISN'T LONG BEFORE THE WORD IS OUT!

IMAGINE! A **TALKING** BIRD!

THEY SAY IT'S A REGULAR **JABBERBOX**!

MAYBE IT'LL GIVE UP AND RUN FOR OFFICE!

HEY! THE ZOOLOGICAL SOCIETY HAS UPPED THE REWARD TO **$5000**!

NO WONDER DUCKBURG WOODS IS BEGINNING TO LOOK LIKE DOWNTOWN AT RUSH HOUR!

THAT BIRD IS GOING TO HAVE A TOUGH TIME HIDING OUT NOW! HEH! HEH!

CRIMINEY ON TOAST! NOW EVERYBODY THINKS **I'M** THE BIRD!

I GUESS IT'S TIME TO THROW IN THE TOWEL, GET OUT OF THIS COSTUME AND GO **HOME**!

OH, GREAT! THE LAME-BRAINED ZIPPER IS **JAMMED**! NOW WHAT DO I DO?

TUG TUG

IF I HANG AROUND HERE, ONE OF THOSE GREEDY HYENAS WILL NAIL ME FOR SURE! I NEED SOMEPLACE TO HIDE UNTIL NIGHTFALL, THEN MAYBE I CAN **SNEAK** HOME!

—*HUFF! PUFF!*— STOP, PEGGY! WE DON'T WANT ANYONE TO SEE YOU!

IT'S FOR YOUR OWN GOOD!

MOMMY! LOOK!

CLOP! *CLOP!* *CLOP!*

D 2002-113

A HORSIE WITH WINGS JUST RUNNED BY!

YOU'RE SUPPOSED TO DO YOUR *DREAMING* IN BED, SWEETIE!

IT'S BEEN A GREAT EVENING, OL' PAL, BUT IT'S TIME TO HEAD HOME!

HEY, DO YOU SEE WHAT I SEE?

CAFÉ

YEAH! A TAXI AT THE CORNER!

NEVER MIND! I MUST BE SEEING THINGS!

CLOP! *CLOP!*

THERE SHE GOES!

IT'S WORKING! WE'RE SHEPHERDING HER INTO THE PARK!

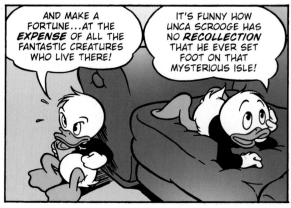

"HOW CAN HE HAVE FORGOTTEN THAT HE FOUND A MAP THAT LED US TO AN ISLAND WHICH EMERGED FROM THE MIDDLE OF A FOGBANK?"

"CAN ALL THE STRANGE MYTHOLOGICAL BEINGS WE MET THERE REALLY HAVE SLIPPED HIS MIND?"

"HAS HE REALLY FORGOTTEN THAT HE SAVED OUR LITTLE PEGASUS WHEN THE CLIFFS STARTED TO CRUMBLE?"

"AND HOW WE MADE A QUICK GETAWAY IN OUR BOAT, TO AVOID BEING CRUSHED, JUST BEFORE WE LOST THE ISLAND IN THE FOG?"

HE NEVER KNEW THAT PEGGY STOWED AWAY ON THE BOAT, BUT WHY HAS HE FORGOTTEN THE REST? HIS MEMORY LOSS IS A MYSTERY!

THE DOORBELL? AT *THIS* HOUR?

Ding Dong!

UH-OH! *RED* ALERT! IT'S UNCA SCROOGE!

C'MON, PEG! WE KNOW YOU'RE *SLEEPY* BUT YOU'VE GOTTA HIDE!

HIYA, UNCLE SCROOGE! DROPPED BY FOR A CUP OF MIDNIGHT COCOA?

DON'T BE SILLY, DONALD! I JUST HAD A BRAINSTORM! AND YOU'RE GOING TO HELP WITH MY NEW SECRET PROJECT...

...PEGASUS!

≥GASP!≤

WHAT?!

I'VE BEEN HAVING WEIRD DREAMS LATELY, NEPHEWS! DREAMS OF A LITTLE FLYING HORSE!

‐GLEEP!‐

I TOOK IT AS AN OMEN! THAT'S WHY I'M CALLING MY NEW *AIRLINE*...PEGASUS!

OH! AN AIRLINE!

PHEW!

GREAT HONK! WHAT ARE YOU KEEPING UPSTAIRS? *ELEPHANTS?*

BUMP! BUMP!

THAT? UH... IT'S ONLY HUEY! HE'S DOING HIS...UM... HOMEWORK... EH...ON THE *TRAMPOLINE!*

N-NOW WE ALL NEED TO GO TO BED! G'NIGHT, UNCLE SCROOGE!

I'LL PICK YOU UP BRIGHT AND EARLY, DONALD!

BUMP! BUMPETY- BUMP!

HOLD IT, PEGGY! UHF! OUCH!

RELAX! THE COAST IS CLEAR! HE'S GONE!

WHY'S SHE SO FIRED UP *THIS* TIME?

CLIP! CLOP!

SHE GOT ALL *GIDDY* WHEN SHE HEARD UNCA SCROOGE'S VOICE!

I THINK SHE'S GOT A *CRUSH* ON HIM!

UNCA SCROOGE MAY BE ABSENT-MINDED...

...BUT *YOU'LL* NEVER FORGET HOW HE SAVED YOUR LIFE, WILL YA, PEG?

THE NEXT MORNING...

BOY OH BOY! IS PEG *RESTLESS!* SHE NEEDS EXERCISE, FOR SURE!

UNCA DONALD'S LEFT WITH UNCA SCROOGE ALREADY!

THEN WE'RE ON OUR OWN! LET'S TAKE PEG TO THE COUNTRYSIDE! WE CAN CATCH A BUS OUT OF TOWN!

COME ON, PEGGY! YOU'LL LIKE IT ONCE WE GET THERE!

DOGS ARE ALLOWED ON THE BUS! BUT I THINK THE DRIVER MIGHT *OBJECT* TO A WINGED HORSE!

FRESH MOUNTAIN AIR! THICK PINE FOREST! WE SHOULD HAVE PLENTY OF ROOM TO RUN AROUND WITHOUT BEING SEEN!

WHAT A COINCIDENCE...

THIS OLD BI-PLANE WILL MAKE A SURE-FIRE ATTENTION GRABBER FOR THE OPENING OF MY AIRLINE!

BUT *WHY* DO WE HAVE TO DRIVE ALL THE WAY TO PINE CREEK TO REGISTER THE COMPANY?

BECAUSE PINE CREEK IS THE ONLY DISTRICT ISSUING NEW AIRLINE LICENSES! AND THEY'VE ONLY GOT *ONE!*

YOU'RE *RIGHT,* MCDUCK! AND I'M GONNA BEAT YOU TO IT!

-=GASP!=- *FLINTHEART GLOMGOLD!*

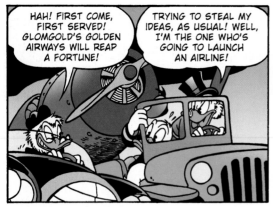

PEGGY! WAIT!

VROOOM!

AWP! WHAT'RE YOU TERMITES *DOING* HERE?

LET'S SAVE THE EXPLANATIONS FOR LATER!

CUSHLA-MACREE! I JUMPED THE GUN!

THIS PLANE WAS NEVER SUPPOSED TO LEAVE THE GROUND!

I'M LOSING ALTITUDE! ⇒GULP!⇐ FAST!

KUH-*RAAASH!!*

GRUNCH!

SKREEEEEEEE!

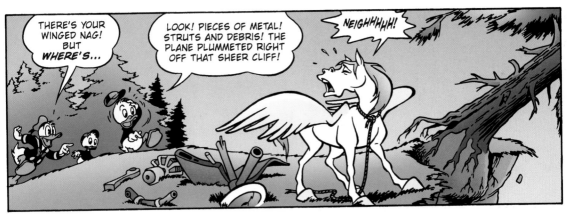

STRANGE! AS SOON AS THE FOG ENVELOPED IT, I FORGOT ALL ABOUT THAT ISLAND!

BUT THE SECOND I SAW THIS LITTLE GAL, IT ALL CAME BACK TO ME!

I GET IT! PEGGY'S THE REASON *OUR* MEMORIES OF THE ADVENTURE REMAINED INTACT!

WE HID HER FROM YOU, UNCA SCROOGE! WE WERE *AFRAID* YOU'D EXPLOIT HER!

NO DANGER OF THAT NOW! I OWE HER—BIG TIME!

MAYBE YOU'D EVEN CONSIDER HELPING HER GET *HOME?*

HEY! LOOKS LIKE PEGGY'S EAGER FOR ANOTHER FLIGHT!

FLAP! FLAP! FLAP!

MAYBE SHE'S STRONG ENOUGH TO CARRY ALL THREE OF US!

SHE IS...

BE CAREFUL, BOYS! AND DON'T FLY TOO FAR AWAY!

WE WON'T...

...WE *THINK!*

AFTER ALL, IT'S PRETTY MUCH UP TO *PEGGY!*

© 2005 Disney
Enterprises Inc.

The Life and Times
of
$crooge McDuck
by
Don Rosa

We all wonder how Carl Barks' webfooted tycoon acquired his famous fortune—and in *Uncle Scrooge* 285-296 (1994-96), modern-day duck maestro Don Rosa told us in a legendary epic serial. From Scrooge's Scottish childhood to his worldwide quest for gold; from his ill-starred love life to his meetings with history's heroes, Rosa left no stone unturned, no penny unpinched. And now Gemstone Publishing is collecting all twelve Eisner-winning chapters in one 264-page trade paperback, annotated by Rosa himself and embellished with art never before seen in the United States. Look for it this June at your favorite book store or comic shop; at just $16.99, it's a deal even a tightwad could love.

WALT DISNEY'S

MINNIE MOUSE

and

CLARABELLE COW

in

REPORTER'S LUCK

CLARA, WOULD YOU LIKE TO ... OH, EXCUSE ME!

OH, THANK YOU, MR. PLATEN! THANK YOU!

YIPPEE! FAREWELL TO A LIFE OF DULL, DREARY, DOMESTIC DRUDGERY!

CLICK!

?

I'M ENTERING INTO A LIFE OF GLAMOR! EXCITEMENT! ROMANCE!

WH-WHAT?

MINNIE, GUESS WHAT! MR. PLATEN, EDITOR OF THE WEEKLY PAPER, HAS MADE ME A ROVING REPORTER!

YOU SURE YOU DON'T MEAN A *RAVING* REPORTER?

OH, TUSH! I'M GOING OUT ON MY FIRST ASSIGNMENT! WANT TO COME ALONG?

WELL, I WAS GOING TO THE PETUNIA SHOW, BUT THIS SOUNDS MORE EXCITING!

LET'S SEE...NOTEBOOK, PENCILS...AND OH, YES... PRESS CARD!

THERE! ALL SET!

WHAT'S YOUR ASSIGNMENT?

OH, THE WHOLE TOWN IS MY BEAT, AS REPORTERS SAY! I JUST GO AROUND AND LOOK FOR NEWS!

HMM! AND SUPPOSE THERE *ISN'T* ANY NEWS?

WHY, MINNIE! WE REPORTERS HAVE AN *INSTINCT* FOR FINDING NEWS! LOTS OF THINGS GO ON AROUND HERE THAT THE AVERAGE PERSON DOESN'T EVEN NOTICE!

?

YOU MEAN LIKE THAT SHED BURNING OVER THERE?

HUH? HUH? WHAT?

FIRE ALARM

WHY, CERTAINLY! SEE WHAT I MEAN? COME ON!

I'LL TURN IN THE ALARM!

PRE

DEAR ME! HERE'S A BUCKET OF WATER! WHY DON'T I TRY AND PUT THE FIRE OUT?

I CAN SEE THE STORY NOW! "DARING REPORTER HELPS PUT OUT FIERCE FIRE"!

I MIGHT EVEN GET MY NAME IN THE PAPER!

FWOOM!

GRACIOUS!

?

WHAT HAPPENED?

I-I DON'T KNOW! I THREW A BUCKET OF WATER, AND FWOOM!

YOU MEAN, YOU THREW THAT BUCKET OF PAINT THINNER?

OH, FOR GOODNESS' SAKES! I DIDN'T NOTICE THAT!

PAINT THINNER

OH, DON'T WORRY! HERE COMES THE FIRE DEPARTMENT!

WHEEEEE

ER... LET'S GO!

PRESS

AREN'T YOU GOING TO STICK AROUND AND GET THE FACTS FOR YOUR STORY?

I DON'T THINK THE FACTS WOULD LOOK SO GOOD IN PRINT!

I CAN SEE THE STORY NOW! "STUPID REPORTER HELPS BURN DOWN SHED!"

I SEE YOUR POINT!

PRESS

OH, WELL! REPORTERS AREN'T SUPPOSED TO BE FIREMEN, ANYWAY! DON'T BE DISCOURAGED!

YOU'RE RIGHT! I'VE LEARNED AN IMPORTANT LESSON!

PRESS

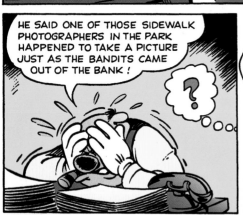

"THE BANDITS WERE CAPTURED THROUGH A TIP GIVEN BY A GAS STATION ATTENDANT WHO RECOGNIZED THEM FROM A DESCRIPTION WHICH APPEARED IN AN EARLIER EDITION OF THIS PAPER!"

WHY, THAT WAS *MY* STORY!

" TWO OF THE BANDITS HAD FALSE BEARDS AND WERE DRIVING A RED CONVERTIBLE WITH A GREEN, YELLOW, BLACK, AND BLUE PLAID TOP!"

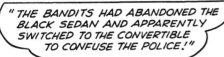

"THE BANDITS HAD ABANDONED THE BLACK SEDAN AND APPARENTLY SWITCHED TO THE CONVERTIBLE TO CONFUSE THE POLICE!"

PLOP!

CLARABELLE!

LATER...

YOU'RE A HEROINE, CLARABELLE! LISTEN! "BRILLIANT DEDUCTING BY REPORTER..."

(PSHAW!) IT WAS *PURE LUCK* AND YOU KNOW IT!

MATTER OF FACT, I'VE RESIGNED FROM THE PAPER! I DECIDED TO RETURN TO THE DOMESTIC LIFE!

REALLY?

YEP! I FIGURE IT'S BETTER TO PRESS CLOTHES THAN PRESS MY LUCK!

COMING IN AUGUST 2005

WALT DISNEY's
MICKEY MOUSE
meets
BLOTMAN

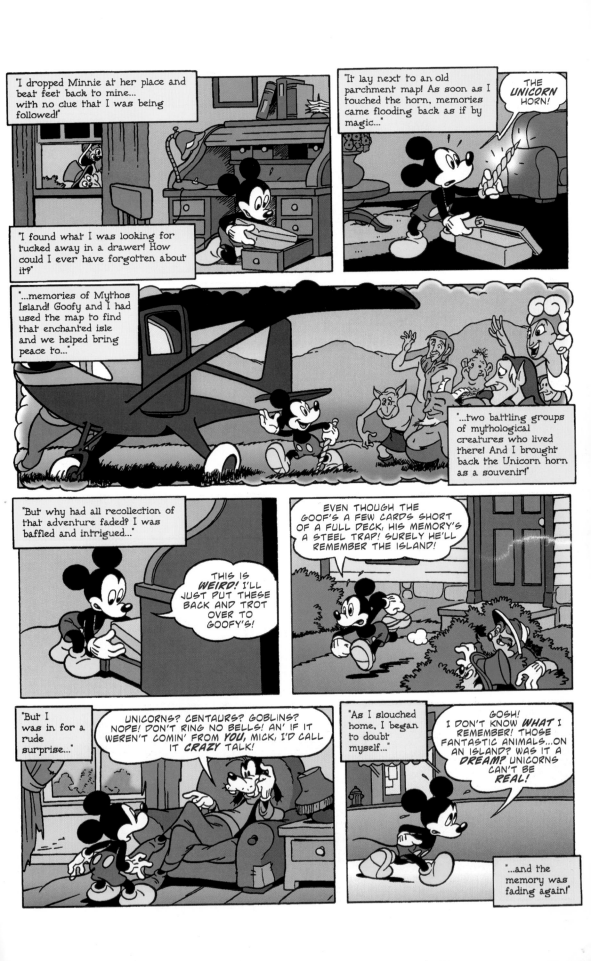

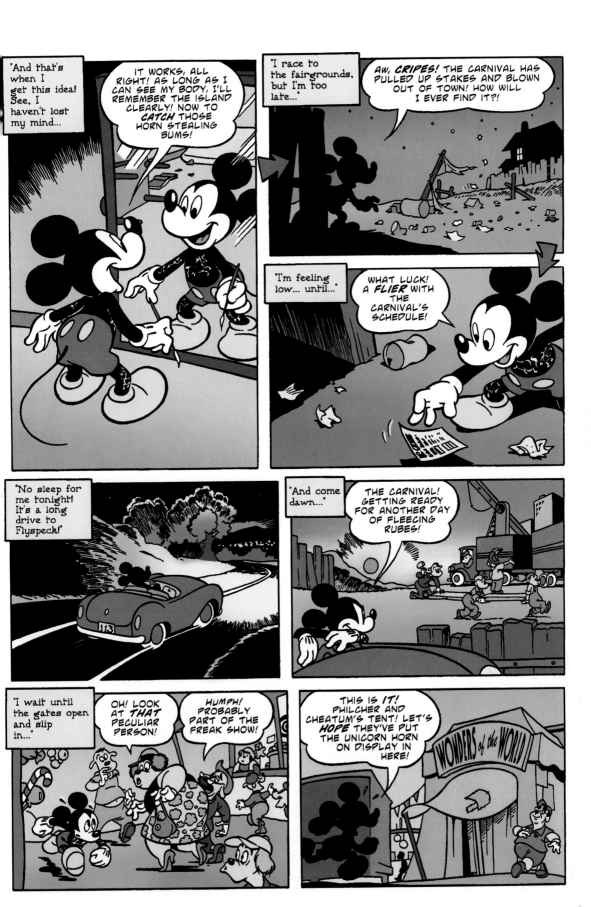

THE SIDESHOW ISN'T OPEN FOR BUSINESS YET! BETTER LUCK FOR ME!

RATS! NO SIGN OF THE HORN *OR* THE MAP! THOSE SKUNKS MUST REALIZE THEY'RE TOO *GOOD* FOR THEIR CHEESY TOURIST TRAP!

HEY, YOU! DO YOU BELONG IN HERE?

-KRYPTONITE-

JEEPERS, KID! YOU STARTLED ME OUT OF MY SKIN!

YOU SNUCK IN TOO? GEE! I FIGGERED *YOU* WAS THE TATTOOED MAN!

-KRYPTO

ME? NAH! I *PAINTED* THIS STUFF ON ME TO HELP ME REMEMBER!

REMEMBER *WHAT?*

A *WONDERFUL*, MAGICAL ISLAND WHERE UNBELIEVABLE CREATURES LIVE! FAIRIES! GOBLINS! CENTAURS AND TROLLS! THAT'S RIGHT! THEY'RE *REAL!*

THEY *ARE?!*

YOU BET! AND WE MUST *NEVER* STOP BELIEVING IN THEM! *YOU* KNOW WHAT I MEAN, DON'T YOU?

SURE! I WONDER...

...WHY A *NUT* LIKE YOU IS ALLOWED LOOSE WITHOUT A *KEEPER!*

HOW D'YA LIKE *THAT?* KIDS THESE DAYS ARE SUCH *CYNICS!*

WELL, LET THE LITTLE TWERP *WALLOW* IN HIS COMPUTER GAME REALITY! I'VE GOT TO—EH?!

ALL WE'VE GOT TO DO IS CHARTER A BOAT AND WALTZ ONTO THAT ISLAND!

AND WHEN WE *DO*, WE'LL NAB AN ATTRACTION THAT'LL KNOCK THE SUCKERS' *SOCKS* OFF!

THOSE CRUDS WILL *RUIN* THE ISLAND IF THEY FIND IT! HOW THE HECK DO I STOP THEM?

PERFORMER'S WARDROBE

SAY! IT'S FULL OF COSTUMES AND MAKE-UP! *JUST* WHAT I NEED!

HERE'S TO OUR PLAN! IT'LL MAKE US *RICH!*

DON'T GET UP, GENTLEMEN! IT'S JUST ME, THE BEARDED LADY! I'M LOOKING FOR... EH... MY ELECTRIC *TRIMMER!* HAVE YOU SEEN IT?

THIS IS A *PRIVATE* TRAILER, MADAM! GET OUT!

EXACTLY WHAT I WANT TO DO! AS SOON AS I *FIND* MY RAZOR!

SHEESH! I CAN'T SEE MY *BODY* IN THIS OUTFIT! IT'S SECONDS BEFORE I FORGET WHAT I'M AFTER! MY MIND'S GETTING *FUZZY* ALREADY!

AH! I *BELIEVE* I LEFT IT IN THIS BOX! THANKS, GENTS, AND TOODLE-OO!

AWP! *STOP* HER!

≥GASP!≤ IT'S THE *RODENT!* GET HIM!

TOO LATE, BOZOS! I'M *HISTORY!*

RRRRIP!

OH NO! THE ONLY THING IN THIS BOX IS THE *MAP!* WHERE'S THE *FURSHLUGINER* UNICORN HORN?!

YOU WON'T ELUDE US, MOUSE!

IF I AT LEAST CAN KEEP THOSE SKUNKS FROM GETTING THEIR MITTS BACK ON THE MAP, THEY'LL NEVER *FIND* THE ISLAND!

"But I wanted the horn back, too! What a fix! How to turn the tables on these rascals?"

BETTER DUCK IN HERE! IT'S MY BEST CHANCE!

OR *IS* IT? THIS CRAZY PLACE IS ONLY SLOWING ME DOWN!

TTHHEERREE'SS GGOOTTTTAA BBEE AA BBEETTTTEERR WWAAYY OOFF DDEEAALLIINNGG WWIITTHH BBAADD GGUUYYSS TTHHAANN TTHHIISS!!

WHOOO-EEE! *THAT'S* MORE LIKE IT! WONDER WHERE THIS SLIDE LEADS?

AW, CRIPES! A DARK CHAMBER! IF I CAN'T SEE THE PICTURES ON MY BODY, I'LL *FORGET* ABOUT THE ISLAND!

MOUSE? WE *KNOW* YOU'RE HERE! GIVE IT UP!

NO WAY! BUT... UH... *WHY* ARE YOU CHASING ME?

JUST HAND THE MAP OVER AND WE WON'T —

WHOLP!

HE BACKED INTO A CHUTE! AFTER HIM!

SOME GAMES ARE PLAYED JUST FOR FUN, OTHERS FOR THE CHALLENGE! THEN THERE'S THE KIND ONLY GOOFY PLAYS—

I DON'T *UNNERSTAND* IT, GILBERT! I'VE GOT PRACTICALLY *EVERY* GAME IN THUH KNOWN *UNIVERSE*, BUT YUH DON'T LIKE *ANY* OF 'EM?

THEY'RE TOO *SIMPLE*, UNCLE GOOFY! THEY JUST DON'T HOLD ANY *OOMPH* FOR A MIND LIKE MINE!

D 2000-014

I'D *GLADLY* PLAY A GAME IF IT WERE *INTELLECTUALLY STIMULATING!*

WELL, WE GOTTA FIND *SOMETHIN'* TA DO WHILE YER VISITIN'!

PERHAPS A MODIFIED *HIDE AND SEEK!* I'LL HIDE—AND LEAVE A TRAIL OF *DEVIOUS CLUES* LEADING YOU TO MY LOCATION!

TERRIFIC! I'LL PUT THIS STUFF AWAY WHILE *YOU* COME UP WITH THEM *CLUES!*

HMM!

MY UNCLE IS A FINE SPORT, BUT NO MATCH FOR MY KEEN BRAIN! THE REAL *CHALLENGE* IS TO WRITE CLUES *EASY* ENOUGH FOR HIM TO FOLLOW!

MUCH, MUCH LATER—

>SIGH!< I ADMIT IT! I *AM* LICKED! AT LEAST I FOUND A *COMFY* PLACE TO REST MUH WEARY *BONES!*

SAY! BEIN' COMFY MAKES THIS BENCH PRETTY *USEFUL!* I WONDER...

>HAW!< LOOK *HERE!* A BIG FAT *GIFT CERTIFICATE* FOR *HARRY'S HASH AN' BURGERS!*

MUST BE GILBERT'S WAY OF SAYIN' HE'LL BE *FOUND* BACK *HOME,* WAITIN' FOR *DINNER...*

...AN' HE MUST WANT *GUESTS!* THIS CERTIFICATE'S ENOUGH TA FEED AN ARMY!

IT'S BEEN *FOUR HOURS!* EVEN *UNCLE GOOFY* SHOULD HAVE LOCATED ME BY *NOW!* I WONDER IF HE'S BACK HERE—

GILBERT! *FOUND* YUH!

UNCLE GOOFY! *WHAT?!*

I ADMIT THERE WAS SOME *TOUGH GOIN'* THERE, GILBERT—BUT I *WON!* YUH MUST NOT BE AS SMART AS YUH THINK!

HULK ™

ALEX ROSS MINI HEAD BUST

DIAMOND SELECT TOYS & DYNAMIC FORCES, INC. HAVE JOINED FORCES TO PRESENT THIS COOL, AFFORDABLE COLLECTIBLE BASED ON **DYNAMIC FORCES'** FULL-SIZED **HULK**™ BUST. DESIGNED BY **ALEX ROSS** AND SCULPTED BY **MIKE HILL**, THIS BUST MEASURES APPROXIMATELY **5" TALL** AND WILL BE THE PRIDE OF YOUR COLLECTION! INCLUDES HAND-NUMBERED, FULL-COLOR CERTIFICATE OF AUTHENTICITY AS WELL AS **NUMBERING** ON THE BOX AND THE PIECE ITSELF!

IN STORES MARCH 2005! AVAILABLE FOR ORDER NOW IN THE MARVEL SECTION!

www.marvel.com

www.diamondselecttoys.com

DYNAMICFORCES.COM

COMIC SHOP LOCATOR SERVICE
888-COMIC-BOOK

DONALD HAS A NEW JOB AT UNCLE SCROOGE'S USED CAR LOT!

PHOOEY! WASH, WASH— ALL I DO IS WASH! WHEN UNCLE SCROOGE TOLD ME I HAD A SHINING FUTURE, I DIDN'T THINK HE MEANT MAKING JALOPIES SPARKLE!

D 2001-136

WIPE THE WINDOWS, POLISH THE BODY, BURNISH THE CHROME...

HEY, DUCK! GET A MOVE ON! WE AIN'T PAYIN' YA TA LOAF!

?!

AND WHEN YOU'RE THROUGH OUTSIDE, WASH THE CARS IN THE SHOWROOM!

YESSIR! YESSIR!

≠Hmm!≠ TWO DIRT SPECKS! I DON'T WANNA SEE ANY!

BUT WITH THE FIVE ON THE FENDER, THEY MAKE A LUCKY SEVEN!

HE DOESN'T *LOOK* SICK! HE RAN OVER HERE AT A MILE A MINUTE...

HAW! A MAN *NEVER* LOOK SICK WHEN HE GOT *EAST GEORGIAN WEASELS!* BUT DAT ONLY *PROVES* HE NEED *MEDICINE* ALL TH' MORE!

HELP US GIT THERE, BOY! A *SECOND'S* DELAY COULD BE *UTTER* DEE-BILITATIN'!

I PRAY THEE, O KNIGHT! WE MUST HASTEN! WE MUST NOT LET ANYTHING HINDER US!

FEAR NOT, MY LADY! I'LL TAKE YOU TO THE GOOSETOWN CAR LO— I MEAN, HOSPITAL! YOUR SON SHALL RISE AGAIN!

NAUGHT HALTS THE HEROISM OF... WHAT'D HE CALL ME?... *SIR WASHALOT!*

VROOOOOM!

NO ROAD TOO LONG! NO FIELD TOO BUMPY!

THUMP!

BOOMP!

AND SHOULD MY STEED BREAK DOWN, NOSEPIERRE, I'LL *CARRY* YOU ON *FOOT!* EVEN IF THE JOURNEY IS A FORTY-MILE SLOG!

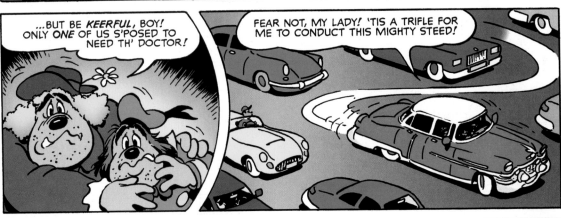

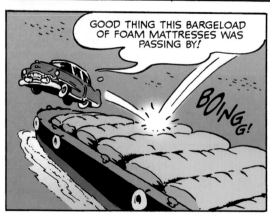

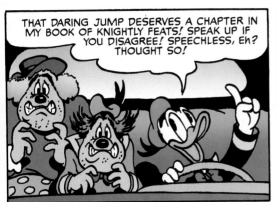